FUNBARRASSING

FUNBARRASSING

Other books by
Shawn L. McMaster

FUNBARRASSING 2
50
Moments That Will
Probably NOT
Happen to
You!

FUNBARRASSING 50

Funny and Embarrassing Moments That Will Probably Happen to You!

Shawn L. McMaster

FUNBARRASSING

Copyright © 2023 Shawn L McMaster
All rights reserved
ISBN:979-8-218-27692-8

FUNBARRASSING

Special thanks to my family, friends, and all the funny and embarrassing moments that happen in life!

FUNBARRASSING

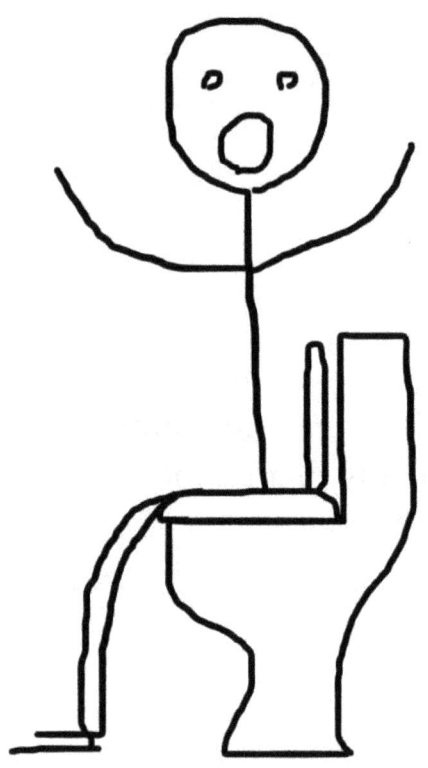

FUNBARRASSING

#1
You will probably realize there is no toilet paper after going #2!

FUNBARRASSING

FUNBARRASSING

#2
You will probably accidentally fart really loud in public!

FUNBARRASSING

FUNBARRASSING

#3
You will probably step in a puddle that is deeper than expected!

FUNBARRASSING

FUNBARRASSING

#4
You will probably smile in front of somebody and have food in your teeth!

FUNBARRASSING

FUNBARRASSING

#5
You will probably have a bad hair day!

FUNBARRASSING

FUNBARRASSING

#6
You will probably experience a bad handshake or hug!

FUNBARRASSING

#7
You will probably fall or trip in public!

FUNBARRASSING

FUNBARRASSING

#8
You will probably call someone the wrong name!

FUNBARRASSING

FUNBARRASSING

#9
Someone will probably call you the wrong name!

FUNBARRASSING

FUNBARRASSING

#10
You will probably forget someone's name!

FUNBARRASSING

FUNBARRASSING

#11
You will probably put your shoes on the wrong feet!

FUNBARRASSING

FUNBARRASSING

#12
You will probably go to the bathroom at someone else's house and the toilet won't flush!

FUNBARRASSING

FUNBARRASSING

#13
You will probably step in dog poop!

FUNBARRASSING

FUNBARRASSING

#14
You will probably get out of the shower and realize there is still some soap on your body!

FUNBARRASSING

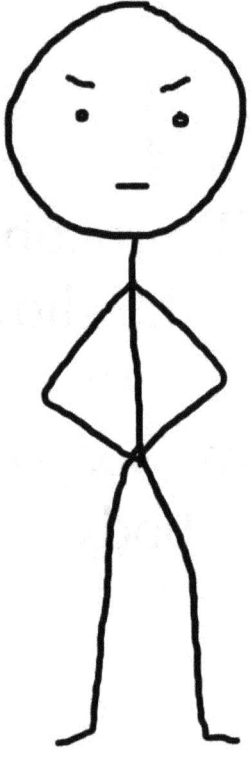

FUNBARRASSING

#15
You will probably get out of the shower and realize that you do not have a towel!

FUNBARRASSING

FUNBARRASSING

#16
You will probably pull someone's finger!

FUNBARRASSING

FUNBARRASSING

#17
You will probably get pooped on by a bird!

FUNBARRASSING

FUNBARRASSING

#18
You will probably walk into a sliding glass or screen door!

FUNBARRASSING

#19
You will probably be watched by someone that is people watching!

FUNBARRASSING

FUNBARRASSING

#20
You will probably swallow a bug!

FUNBARRASSING

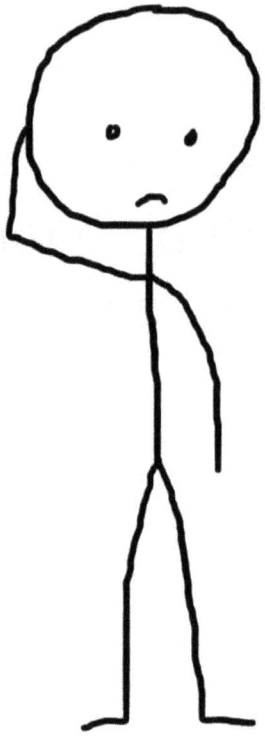

FUNBARRASSING

#21
You will probably wake up in the morning and regret the night before!

FUNBARRASSING

FUNBARRASSING

#22
You will probably smell a bad fart!

FUNBARRASSING

FUNBARRASSING

#23
You will probably have an exposed booger!

FUNBARRASSING

FUNBARRASSING

#24
You will probably get hit in the head with a ball!

FUNBARRASSING

FUNBARRASSING

#25
You will probably spill a drink on someone!

FUNBARRASSING

FUNBARRASSING

#26
You will probably get caught picking your nose!

FUNBARRASSING

FUNBARRASSING

#27
You will probably wave to someone you think is someone else!

FUNBARRASSING

#28
You will probably use someone else's toothbrush by accident!

FUNBARRASSING

FUNBARRASSING

#29
You will probably have food on your face and not know it!

FUNBARRASSING

FUNBARRASSING

#30
You will probably
pull a push door
or vice versa!

FUNBARRASSING

FUNBARRASSING

#31
You will probably have someone tell you that your zipper is down!

FUNBARRASSING

#32
You will probably talk on the phone for a while after it has disconnected!

FUNBARRASSING

#33
You will probably answer someone from another room and then realize they're talking on the phone!

FUNBARRASSING

FUNBARRASSING

#34
You will probably
sit on the toilet
with the seat
up!

FUNBARRASSING

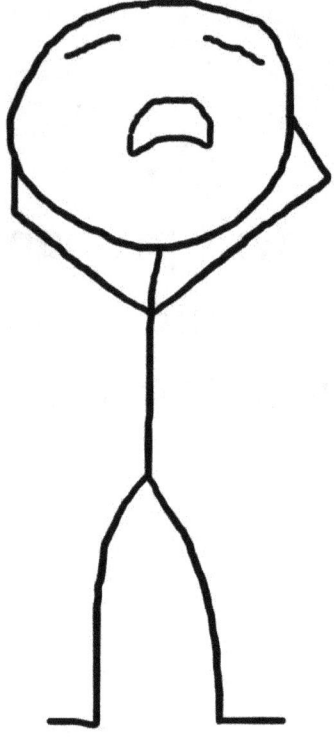

FUNBARRASSING

#35
You will probably
not have clean underwear
due to forgetting to
do your laundry
the day before!

FUNBARRASSING

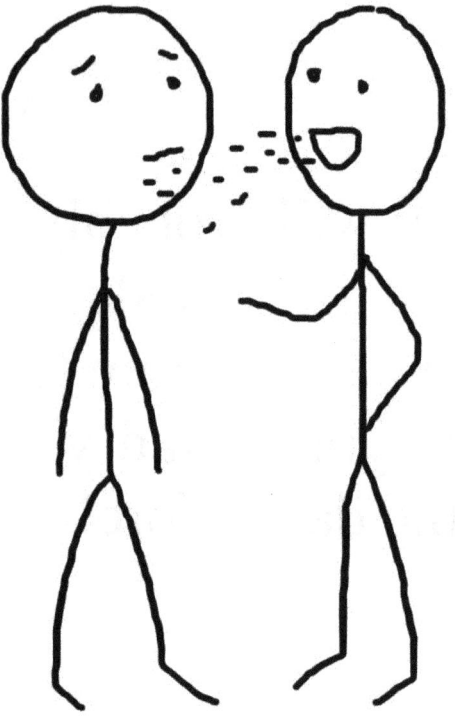

#36
You will probably experience a spit talker!

FUNBARRASSING

FUNBARRASSING

#37
You will probably experience a close talker!

FUNBARRASSING

#38
You will probably talk with someone who has very bad breath!

FUNBARRASSING

FUNBARRASSING

#39
You will probably text the wrong person an embarrassing message!

FUNBARRASSING

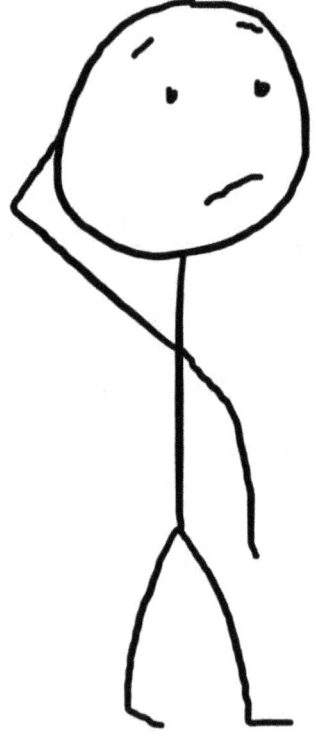

FUNBARRASSING

#40
You will probably show up somewhere the wrong day or time!

FUNBARRASSING

#41
You will probably sleep at another place and wake up wondering where you're at!

FUNBARRASSING

FUNBARRASSING

#42
You will probably call the wrong number!

FUNBARRASSING

FUNBARRASSING

#43
You will probably accidentally wear two different socks!

FUNBARRASSING

FUNBARRASSING

#44
You will probably accidentally wear your shirt inside out!

FUNBARRASSING

FUNBARRASSING

#45
You will probably get poop on your hands!

FUNBARRASSING

FUNBARRASSING

#46
You will probably walk into an occupied bathroom!

FUNBARRASSING

FUNBARRASSING

#47
You will probably drink someone else's drink!

FUNBARRASSING

FUNBARRASSING

#48
You will probably get a prank phone call!

FUNBARRASSING

FUNBARRASSING

#49
You will probably say something about someone and then realize they heard you!

FUNBARRASSING

FUNBARRASSING

#50
You will probably accidentally have an exposed private body part!

FUNBARRASSING

Shawn L. McMaster
is the author of the Funbarrassing
book series. He is both funny, creative,
and clever. He is from and lives in
California.

FUNBARRASSING

www.ingramcontent.com/pod-product-compliance
Lightning Source LLC
Chambersburg PA
CBHW060819050426
42449CB00008B/1726